MONKEY SURPRISE

Andrew Matthews

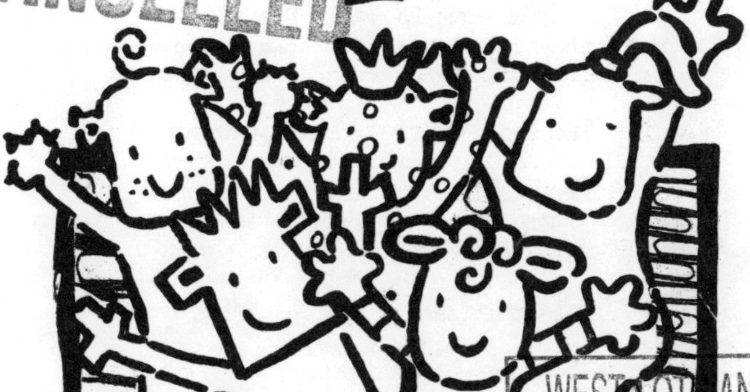

illustrated by
Rebecca Elgar

All stories first published in *Monster Nursery School*
in Great Britain in 1991
by Methuen Children's Books

This edition published in Great Britain in 1998
by Mammoth, an imprint of Reed International Books Limited
Michelin House, 81 Fulham Road, London SW3 6RB

Text copyright © 1991 Andrew Matthews
Illustrations copyright © 1998 Rebecca Elgar

The rights of Andrew Matthews and Rebecca Elgar to be identified as
the author and illustrator of this work have been asserted by them in
accordance with the Copyright, Designs and Patents Act 1988

ISBN 0 7497 3270 9

10 9 8 7 6 5 4 3 2 1

A CIP catalogue record for this book
is available from the British Library

Printed in Great Britain by Cox & Wyman Ltd,
Reading, Berkshire

This paperback is sold subject to the condition that it
shall not, by way of trade or otherwise, be lent, resold,
hired out, or otherwise circulated without the publisher's
prior consent in any form of binding or cover other than
that in which it is published and without a similar
condition including this condition being imposed on
the subsequent purchaser.

Contents

~

1 Baby gets bored
1

2 The Monster's thinking-cap
10

3 The Monster fair
17

4 The playtime pest
24

5 Baby's birthday
35

6 A Monster surprise
43

1 Baby gets bored

After a delicious breakfast of cow and custard, washed down with mugs of hot golden syrup and rhubarb juice, the Monster and Mrs Monster went to work. Soon, the air outside the cave was filled with the sounds of sawing and hammering. The air inside the cave was filled with the sounds of mixing and measuring.

Baby Monster sat at the edge of her cot and twiddled her tentacles. She pressed her rubber duck and made it go BAMP! Then she picked up her favourite picture book. She read it forwards, backwards and upside-down, then she frowned. Deep down inside herself, Baby could feel a tiny, gloomy feeling. 'Trevor!' she smiled. With a flutter of wings she flew down from the cot and went to find Trevor the tiger so that they could play a game together.

But when she found him, he was curled up fast asleep on her parents' monstrous duvet.

'Wake up. Play, Trevor,' said Baby, shaking the bed.

'H-m-o-o-r!' snoozed Trevor. He turned over and went straight back to sleep.

'Oh, bother,' said Baby. She could still feel the gloom deep down inside her, but it wasn't tiny anymore – it had grown small.

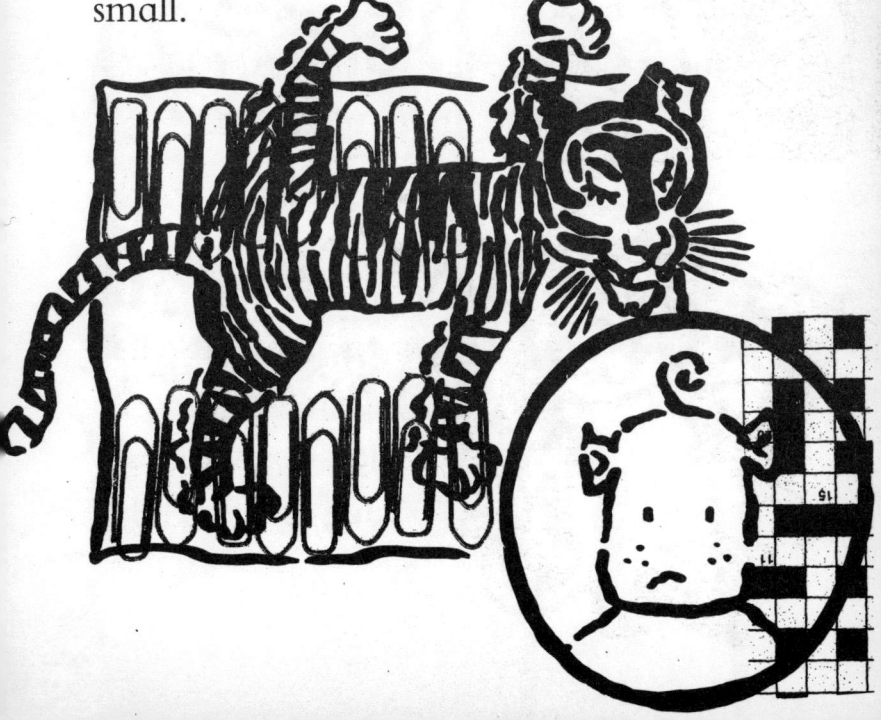

She skipped over to her dad. He was wearing his favourite flowery pinafore. He was cracking eggs with his claws and stirring bowls with spoons held in his tentacles while he hooshed the oven alight with his hot monstery breath.

'I'll help you, Dad,' Baby said happily.

'What?' said the Monster. 'Er . . . I'm afraid not, darling. I've got my claws and tentacles full, and the oven is far too hot for a baby monster to go near. You might burn yourself. I'm sorry, but that's how it is when you're rustling up a wing-ding meal of tip-top monster grub.'

'Oh, bother,' said Baby. The gloom inside her was still there, but instead of being small it had grown to be middle-sized. Baby went outside the cave and followed the short path down to her mother's workshop. Mrs Monster was sawing and sanding and banging nails.

'I'll help you, Mum,' Baby said happily.

'What?' said Mrs Monster. 'Oh, I'm afraid you can't, cutie. You might cut yourself on the saw or bang yourself with the hammer and the wood might give you splinters in your bottoms. I'm sorry, but that's how it is when you're slapping together a set of monstrous shelves.'

'Oh, bother,' said Baby. The gloomy feeling was really quite big now, and instead of being deep down inside, it was nearly right at the top.

Baby's bottom lip trembled. Her fur went green and her tentacles went all droopy.

'W-A-A-H!' she wailed. The hot tears on her face made her head steam.

'Baby!' exclaimed Mrs Monster. 'Are you all right?' She dropped all her tools and picked up Baby to give her a huge monster cuddle.

Mr Monster came running out of the cave to see what was the matter.

Trevor the tiger was close behind him, lashing his tail in a worried way.

They all stood round until Baby had stopped crying enough to explain what was wrong.

'Dad's all busy. Mum's all busy. There's nothing for me to do!'

Mrs Monster looked at the Monster and frowned. 'Mr Monster, our Baby is bored.'

'So she is,' agreed the Monster. 'What she needs is something to do.'

'What she needs,' said Mrs Monster, 'is a place to go where she'll find lots of interesting things to do. A place where there'll be other baby monsters to make friends with. Would you like that, Baby?'

'Ooy,' said Baby, nodding her head so fast that her ears went flippety-flap.

'What place is that then, Mrs Monster?' puzzled the Monster.

'Why, school of course!' said Mrs Monster. 'Baby monsters have a great time in school. They paint pictures, sing songs and play games all day.'

'Want to go to school,' yelled Baby. 'Want to go to school.'

'Er . . . Mrs Monster,' said the Monster, 'can I go to school as well? It sounds like a bit of all right.'

2 The Monster's thinking-cap

Mrs Teacher made her pupils sit at the tables with their tentacles neatly folded. She had a serious expression on her face and her fur had turned dark purple.

'Monsters, I've been thinking,' she said. 'For ages and ages, I've fancied having a monster piano for the school. I could just fit one in that corner over there. If we had a monster piano, it would make our shouting songs sound much better – and you could bounce your bottoms on it as a treat.'

'C-o-r, ye-ah!' said the little monsters.

'The trouble is, we need funds,'

confessed Mrs Teacher.
'We need lots and lots for
a piano but the School
Fund Box hasn't got
a mite left in it.'

'I know, Mrs Teacher,'
cried Mel Monster,
wriggling with excitement.
'We could dress up in masks,
creep up on other monsters
and say, "Give us all your
groats and florins, or we'll
do something really,
really naughty!" '

'I don't think
that's a terribly
good idea, Mel dear,' smiled Mrs Teacher. 'And I don't think your mum and dad would like you to do anything really, really naughty.'

'I would,' chirped Mel.

'What I thought,' said Mrs Teacher, 'is that we could have a Monster Nursery School Fair. There would be lots of running, jumping and flying races and I'm sure your parents would be willing to help us by bringing along things other monsters would want to buy. We could set up lots of stalls.'

'My mum would help make them,' said Baby.

'And I could go in all the running, jumping and flying races and win the lot!' shouted Mel.

The little monsters were extremely excited about Mrs Teacher's idea.

Baby told her mum and dad all about it while they had tea.

'It sounds a spiffulous idea,' said Mrs Monster. 'I've often wanted to knock a few stalls together. Now's my chance, and you could bake some ostrich and onion pies to sell, Mr Monster.'

'No,' the Monster declared. 'This fund-raising lark calls for something super-specially different and scrummy. I'll have to put my thinking-cap on.'

The Monster's thinking-cap was made of wool. It was blue, with yellow flowers on the sides and two holes in the top for his horns to poke through. The Monster pulled it on and sat down next to the oven.

After a bit, Mrs Monster said, 'Any thoughts yet, Mr Monster?'

'Not yet, Mrs Monster,' said the Monster. 'My brain's just started ticking.'

And it had. From under the cap came a noise like a big, old grandfather clock.

After a bit longer, Mrs Monster said, 'How are your thoughts coming along?'

'Starting to roll, Mrs Monster,' replied the Monster. And from underneath his thinking-cap came a noise like the wheels of a train going CLAPPETY-SNICK! SNIKKETY-CLAP!

Suddenly, the Monster bounded into the air.

'YA-HOO!' he roared.
'YIP-EE! YES, INDEEDY.'
'I think your dad's had a good idea,' Mrs Monster told Baby.

The Monster worked at super speed. His arms went round faster than a spin-drier. His tentacles whirled like emptying bath-water.

His hoofs were a blur. He chopped, mixed, measured, stirred, whisked and fried until . . .

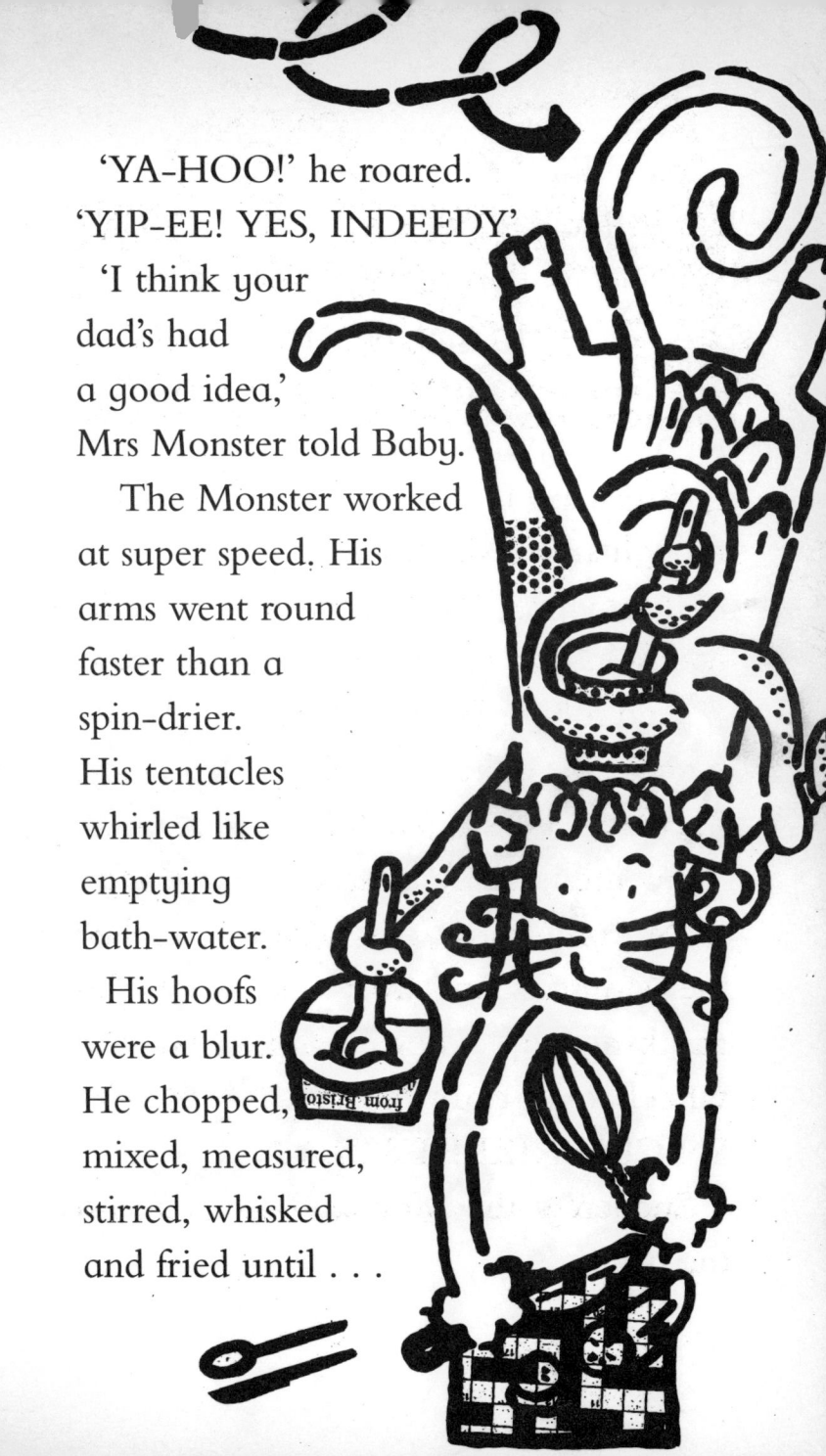

'That's it!' he yelled, holding up a round bun with a dark filling. 'I've invented the bull-and-banana burger.' He took a bite, chewed it carefully and smacked his lips. 'Hmmm!' He frowned. 'Something's not quite right. What this burger needs is a good splodge of a mega-lush, tongue-tickling chutney, and I'm just the monster who can make it.'

3 The Monster Fair

The Monster was off again! He whooshed and whizzed all over the place, making up a song while he worked.

*'Green chilli, red chilli,
Pepper black and white,
Mustard and paprika
And curry – that's right!
Radishes and onions –
Pickled and raw!
And then, to make it really hot,
Just add a little more
Green chilli, red chilli,
Pepper white and black,
To make a proper chutney
For a toothsome monster snack!'*

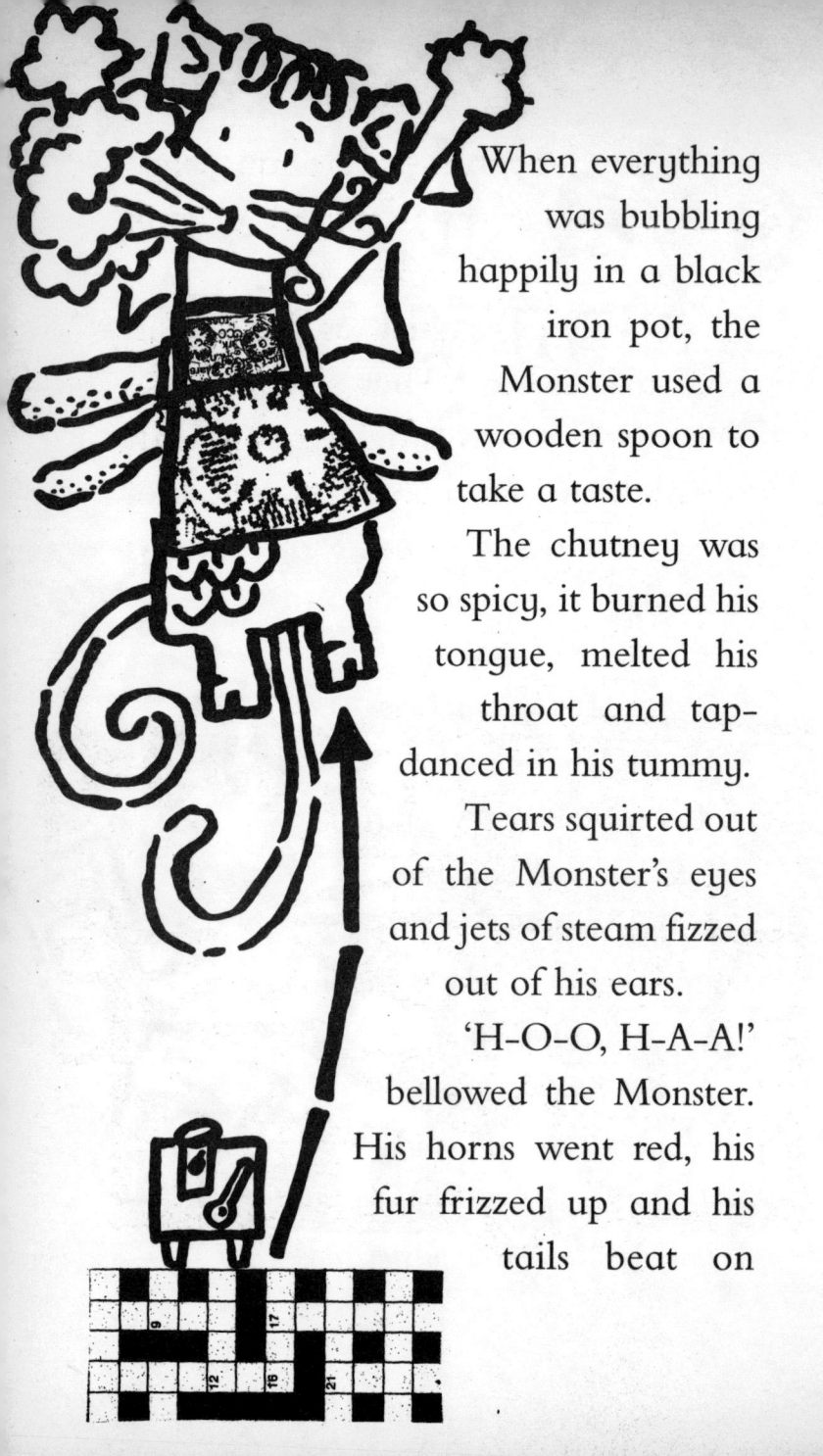

When everything was bubbling happily in a black iron pot, the Monster used a wooden spoon to take a taste.

The chutney was so spicy, it burned his tongue, melted his throat and tap-danced in his tummy.

Tears squirted out of the Monster's eyes and jets of steam fizzed out of his ears.

'H-O-O, H-A-A!' bellowed the Monster. His horns went red, his fur frizzed up and his tails beat on the floor like drumsticks. He ran across the cave, picked up a barrel of rain water and gulped it down.

'A-a-a-h,' he sighed as his tonsils hissed and sizzled. 'That should make the bull-and-banana burgers a bit more lively. If I brew up a few gallons of goozgogade, we should raise bags of funds.'

On the day of the Monster Nursery School Fair the sun shone and a pleasantly cool breeze blew over the lake. All the stalls had been set up in the school garden and the place was packed. Mel Monster entered all the races, but he didn't win any of them.

'It's not fair!' he sulked to Baby.

'You did your best,' Baby told him.

'But all the races were won by girlies!' Mel complained. 'Boy monsters are supposed to be tops at sports.'

'Let's find Trevor,' said Baby. 'He'll lick your face and make you feel better.'

Over at the Monster Burger Bar, the Monster and Mrs Monster were doing a roaring trade. In fact, all the monsters who tasted the Monster's chilli chutney roared. They also hooted, screeched, stamped their hoofs and snorted. They bought so much goozgogade to cool themselves down, that the Monster sold out.

'You'll have to guzzle the lake,' he told his gasping customers.

When the sky grew dark, there was a spectacular hooshing show put on by monster experts who could make lots of different-coloured fire come out of their snouts at the same time.

21

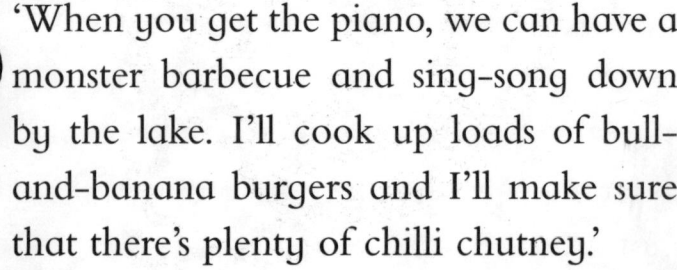

Over fifteen buckets of funds were collected and when they were given to Mrs Teacher, she turned all pink and sniffly. 'Oh dear,' she squeaked as her bottom lip wobbled, 'I don't know how I can thank you all.' 'Easy-peasy,' shouted the Monster. 'When you get the piano, we can have a monster barbecue and sing-song down by the lake. I'll cook up loads of bull-and-banana burgers and I'll make sure that there's plenty of chilli chutney.'

The thought of the Monster's chilli chutney made all the monster experts hoosh at once. The flames rose up into the air like a red fountain.

'I can do that,' yelled Mel. He tried to hoosh, but all he could manage was a dribble of smoke that made him cough and Baby laugh.

'Boy monsters are funny,' giggled baby.

'Oh, bother!' scowled Mel.

4 The playtime pest

Though he behaved badly in class sometimes, it was in the playground that Mel was worst. He was a real playtime pest.

There was always a queue for the slide, but Mel wouldn't wait. He barged and elbowed his way to the front and made sure the others were looking before he slid down. On the swings, Mel loved being pushed, but when it was his turn to push he would run away laughing. Mel didn't join in games with the other little monsters, he tried to take them over, bossing everyone about with his loud, shouty voice.

One day, the other little monsters decided they were well and truly fed up with Mel. When the class went out for morning playtime, Mel clattered straight over to the slide, as usual.
When he got there, much to his surprise he found that there was no queue and that the others were playing on the swings.

'Cor,' he said. 'Hey, look at me everybody. I'm going to go down the slide on my back head-first! Bet you've never seen a monster do that before.'

As soon as he was at the bottom of the slide, he raced back to the top, bawling, 'Watch this then!' But no matter how hard he shouted, the other little monsters paid no attention to him. And Mel did something silly. He stood on his head, right at the top of the slide. He lost his balance, rolled down in a tangle of arms and tentacles and landed – WHOMP! – face down on the playground.

'Funny Mel!' tittered Baby. She was watching what happened from a seat near the rose bushes.

'Slides are pooey anyway,' grumbled Mel as he picked himself up. 'One minute you're on top of a slide, the next minute you're at the bottom. What's so good about that? Slides are for weenie monsters and girlies, not gruff, tough boy monsters like me!'

He clomped over towards the swings. When the others saw Mel coming, they left the swings and went on to the roundabout.

Mel pretended that he didn't care. He sat on a swing and fluttered his wings to help him go back and fore.

'Coo! Hey, look at me, everybody,' he shouted. 'I'm so good at swinging, I don't need anyone else to push me. Just watch this.' He let go with one paw. 'I bet you've never seen a monster go this high on a swing before and I bet you've never seen this.'

And Mel did something really, really silly. He was up very high and he let go with both paws. When the swing swung back, Mel kept on going forwards.

'Oo-er!' he shrieked.
He sailed through the air
and landed – PLUD! –
head first in the
garden compost heap.

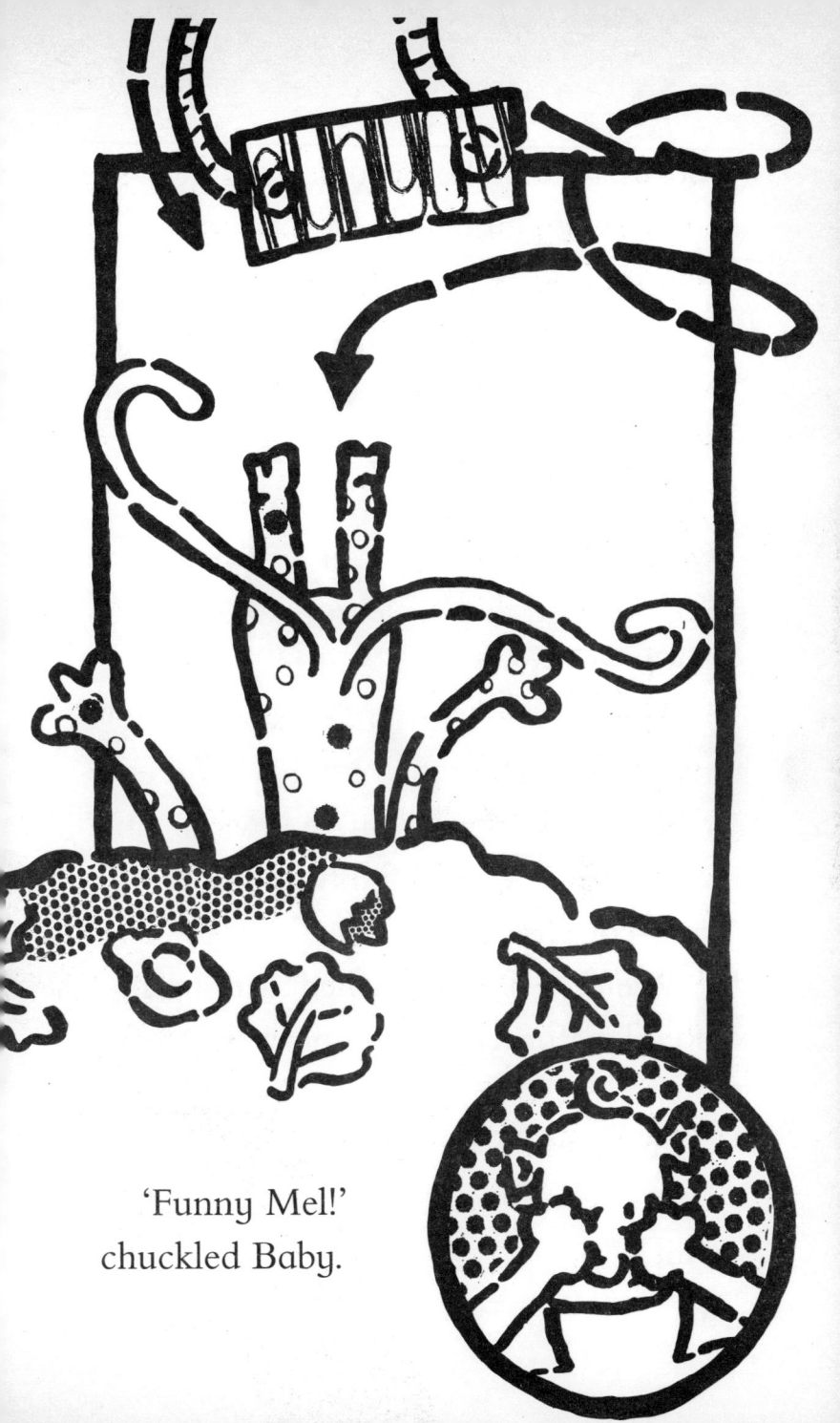

'Funny Mel!' chuckled Baby.

When Mel hauled himself out of the compost heap, Baby was still chuckling, but she couldn't help feeling sorry for him too. There were old cabbage leaves in his fur, bits of egg shell on his scales and a mouldy turnip was stuck to one of his horns.

'That was great!' said Mel, pretending that he hadn't had an accident. 'Jumping off a swing and landing in a heap of rotting rubbish is super-cool fun.'

When Mel approached the roundabout, the others left it and went to the slide.

'Phe-e-e-w!' one of them said loudly. 'That Mel monster smells awful. What a whiff.'

'Well I think I smell lush,' Mel yelled. He took in a deep breath through his snout. 'Mmm, good!' he exclaimed. 'Boy monsters ought to have a good romp in rubbish, it makes them smell hunky.'

He jumped up on to the roundabout. He was feeling miserable, but pretended he was having fun.

'Goody, goody gum-drops. I've got the roundabout all to myself. If you want to see the best way of having fun on a roundabout, watch me.' He jumped down to the ground, pushed as fast as he could and then jumped back on the roundabout while it was still moving. 'Whe-e-e! Look at me go,' Mel bellowed.

But the roundabout was going slowly and it stopped after half a turn. Mel's mouth went all wrinkly. His horns turned yellow and drooped.

'I don't care,' he sulked. 'It's much more fun playing on my own. Girlie monsters are too cissy to play with and the other boy monsters aren't as gruff and tough as I am.'

Mel kicked the side of the roundabout angrily. It went – KA-BONG! – and hurt his hoof.

It was too much for Mel. He sat down on the roundabout and cried and cried. The scalding hot tears steamed and steamed out of his eyes like tea from a teapot. They washed egg shell off his scales and boiled the cabbage leaves in his fur until they went slimy.

Baby hopped down from her seat and walked over. Mel saw her coming and tried to stop crying.

'What do you want?' he snuffled grumpily.

'I want to be your friend, Mel,' said Baby. 'I think you're funny, only . . .'

'Only what?' snapped Mel.

'Only you must stop saying nasty things about girl monsters,' Baby replied. 'You mustn't show off so much and you have to take a bath.'

'Huh!' growled Mel. He used a complaining voice, but there was a twinkle in his eyes. 'Oh, all right! Girl monsters aren't so bad, I suppose, and this rubbish does smell a bit strong. And I do show off all the time. I promise I'll never show off again!'

'Oh!' said Baby. 'You can show off a bit. I like it when you bump into things and fall over.'

The thought of it made her laugh. Mel caught the laugh from Baby and used it to dry away his tears.

5 Baby's birthday

The Monster was flying back to the cave, carrying a big, bulging bag. He flew into a hurricane. Down on the ground, trees were ripped up by their roots and blown away, boulders toppled over and started avalanches in the mountains.

'It's a bit breezy today!' the Monster said.

The Monster flew into a thunderstorm. Thunder boomed. Rain and hail lashed him. A dazzling bolt of lightning struck him – KA-PAM! – and made all his fur stand on end.

'This weather is shocking!' the Monster said.

When the Monster returned to his cave, Mrs Monster hooshed him warm and dry and then they both popped the cauldron on to the stove for mugs of hot golden syrup and rhubarb juice.

'You've brought a lot of things home in that bag, Mr Monster!' said Mrs Monster.

'I've been to the monster sales, Mrs Monster!' said the Monster. 'And I've been thinking. It's Baby's birthday soon. I think it would be a great idea if she had a birthday party with lots of jelly and super-special monster scoff. She could invite all her little monster mates and they could play games and stamp and shout!' The Monster was getting carried away. His wings were whirring like a clockwork mouse. He kept rising into the air and sinking down again. 'We could give her a super-duper do!'

'But, Mr Monster,' said Mrs Monster, 'the cave is too small. It's cosy and snug and just right for three, but if we try to fit many more monsters in, there won't be enough room to peel a prune!'

'Oh, plop!' grumbled the Monster, looking around. 'You're quite right, Mrs Monster, and I've been a bit of a daffy dumpling because I've bought all the things I need to cook for the party.' The Monster huffed and stamped a hoof. 'There must be a way to give Baby a wing-ding birthday knees-up.'

'Do you need your thinking-cap?' asked Mrs Monster.

'I do,' the Monster replied. 'I'm sure that a hot drink and my thinking-cap will give me plenty of ideas.' The Monster pulled on his woolly thinking-cap and paced up and down the cave, sipping at his steaming mug.

Before long, his brain started making noises as it began to work. First it purred like a pleased panther, then it hummed like a happy hornet and then it went BODDLA-BOOM! BODDLA-BOOM! like the beating of a dinosaur's heart.

The Monster jumped up and touched the roof of the cave, roaring, 'WHOOPEE! YEE-HAH! YES-SIREE!'

'Have you had an idea, Mr Monster?' Mrs Monster enquired.

'I've had a humdinger-and-a-half of an idea,' the Monster said gleefully. 'We'll ask Mrs Teacher if we can hold the party at the Monster Nursery School!'

'That's such a good idea, I'm going to give you a big monster kiss,' Mrs Monster told her husband.

'Coo!' The Monster blushed bashfully. 'There's plenty more good ideas where that one came from!'

Mrs Teacher thought it was a splendid plan for Baby to have her birthday party at the school. When Baby heard the news, she bounced up and down in excitement.

'Who are you going to invite?' asked the Monster.

Baby danced around, chanting:

'Min and Mel,
Des and Del,

Eddy, Freddy,
Neddy and Teddy!

Mike and Maureen,
Richard and Doreen,

Johnny, Lonnie,
Donny and Bonny!

Julie and Jim,
Tracy and Tim,

Garry, Harry,
Barry and Larry!

Lionel and Lou,
Sammy and Sue

And Mrs Teacher monster too!'

'Hmm!' the Monster said to himself. 'If I'm going to cook enough grub for that lot, I'd better get cracking right away.'

6 A Monster surprise

For the next few days the Monsters were really busy. Mrs Monster was sawing and sanding and being mysterious about something in her workshop. The Monster was cooking and when Baby came home from nursery school, she helped him. She rolled out the pastry for the ostrich-and-onion pies and the toffee-and-turkey tarts. She packed the owl-and-orange pasties into hampers with the snake-and-pig-meat puddings and she screwed the tops on the jars of chilli chutney.

Baby's favourite part was
helping her dad turn the
jellies out of their moulds.
There were jellies of
all shapes and sizes,
colours and flavours.
There were jelly pigs,
rabbits and starfish,
jelly cars, castles
and spaceships,
all glistening and
glimmering as they
jiggled on their plates.
'Well,' the Monster
declared as he packed
away the last batch of
bison biscuits, 'I reckon
that's the lot, Baby.
I couldn't have done
it all without your help.'
Baby beamed when her dad said this.

But the Monster didn't let Baby help with all the cooking. While Baby was at nursery school, the Monster was baking and icing a secret that he didn't want Baby to know about.

On the evening of Baby's party, the Monster Nursery School had been specially decorated. There were balloons, bits of tinsel and a banner that read:

HAPPY BIRTHDAY BABY-Y-A-A-Y!

As soon as Baby arrived, poppers were popped, streamers streamed and all the little monsters shouted and whistled. To Baby's surprise and delight, right at the front of the crowd waiting to meet her was a familiar figure carrying an umbrella and wearing a hat covered with pineapples.

'Granny!' Baby called excitedly. She leapt up into Granny monster's arms and gave her a huge monstrous hug.

'Gracious me,' gasped Granny. 'Not so hard, or I'll pop my corsets.'

After her hug, Granny played songs on the monster piano and everybody had a good stamp and shout and made a real monster rumpus. When that was finished, the little monsters started squeaking, 'Je-lly! Je-lly!'

'Just calm down,' said the Monster. 'The whole world knows how much monsters like jelly, but it has to be done just right. Get into a line and my lovely wife and myself will make sure you get a jelly each.'

The little monsters got into a buzzing, giggly queue and stepped up to take their jellies. Baby's jelly was a yellow rabbit and Mel got a red starfish. 'I want to go first,' he yelled.

'No, we must all do it at the same time,' said the Monster. 'Are you all ready? After three – ha-one, ha-two, ha-THREE!'

And on the count of three, all the monsters threw jelly at each other.

Granny was splodged by a red jelly octopus. It made her smile. Baby was hit by a green castle – GLUDGE! It made her chuckle.

Mel was gludged
by a purple
spaceship.
It made him
guffaw.

After the jelly, there were running, wrestling, flying games and tiddlywinks. Then everybody sat down to a slap-up meal of tip-top monster grub.

When everyone had eaten just about enough, it was time for Baby's presents. Mrs Monster had made Baby a baby-monster sized pencil-case, big enough for all her pencils, pens and crayons. There was a picture of Trevor the tiger painted on the lid, and when Baby opened it, a little music box inside played:

*'Hi-tiddly-batch-cake,
Brown bread!'*

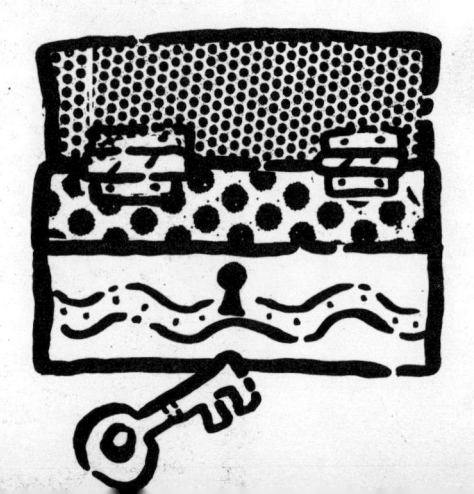

'O-o-y!' went Baby.

'All right,' said the Monster, 'I want you all to close your eyes while I get my present for Baby ready.'

The little monsters sat with their eyes shut tight. There were bumps and squeaks and scrapes.

'Now, open your eyes,' said the Monster.

On a table in the middle of the room stood an enormous birthday cake, decorated to look just like the Monster Nursery School.

'C-o-o-r!' gasped the little monsters.

They were all on the cake. Little marzipan monsters were hanging out of the windows or playing in the playground. A little marzipan Mel was going down the slide head first. Trevor the tiger was peeping round a corner, and in the school doorway stood Mrs Teacher, waving her red, white-spotted handkerchief. Next to her was Granny, holding up her umbrella.

The Monster gave Baby a cake slice. 'You cut the first piece,' he told her.

'Ooh, Dad,' said Baby. 'It's so nice I don't want to cut it.'

'Go on,' Mel shouted naughtily. 'Cut Mrs Teacher's bottoms off!'

If you enjoyed this
MAMMOTH STORYBOOK
look out for:

Monster Mayhem

Andrew Matthews
Illustrated by *Rebecca Elgar*

~

Meet Baby Monster and
her funny family.
There's Mr Monster, Mrs Monster,
Granny Monster and Trevor the tiger.

Mrs Monster has her hands full.
Mr Monster doesn't understand about
looking after children.
He thinks babysitting means he
has to sit on Baby.
Then Baby brings home a rather
unusual pet – a tiger!
Thank goodness Granny Monster's on
hand to sort out the mayhem!

If you enjoyed this
MAMMOTH STORYBOOK
look out for:

Pest Friends

Pippa Goodhart
Illustrated by *Louise Armour-Chelu*

~

Maxine is big and loud
and funny. Minnie is small and
quiet and shy.

And they are best friends –
but don't ask why! At school and
at home, they are never apart.

Then Minnie loses a tooth – and
she's in danger of losing her
best friend too . . .

If you enjoyed this
MAMMOTH STORYBOOK
look out for:

Allie's Apples

Helen Dunmore
Illustrated by *Simone Lia*

~

Allie's big sister can be a perfect pain.
She tells tales and she's always
whispering and laughing behind
Allie's back.

Thank goodness Allie has a best friend
like Misha. Who better to share her
secret – and come up
with a fantastic surprise?

If you enjoyed this
MAMMOTH STORYBOOK
look out for:

Only Molly

Cally Poplak
Illustrated by *Alison Bartlett*

~

Molly is special . . .

One day Molly and her mum
come back from school and find
an unwanted visitor . . .

One day Molly goes out with her
Aunt Jan and something embarrassing
happens – but something
wonderful too . . .

One day Molly and Mum go fishing
with Tim and Rosy and see
something scary . . .

And then Molly is invited to a party . . .
and gets the loveliest surprise of all!

If you enjoyed this
MAMMOTH STORYBOOK
look out for:

Blair the Winner!

Theresa Breslin
Illustrated by *Ken Cox*

~

It's not fair being in the middle,
like Blair.

Little baby Willis is a pest.
Big sister Melissa thinks Blair's
the pest. And all the family
never stop nagging!

But it's Blair who saves
the day on a camping trip
that goes wrong . . .